To my
BELOVED
Suca

Mom

Date:

5-5-14

A HELEN STEINER RICE ® Product

© 2012 by Barbour Publishing, Inc.

All poems © Helen Steiner Rice Foundation Fund, LLC, a wholly owned subsidiary of Cincinnati Museum Center. All rights reserved.

Published under license from the Helen Steiner Rice Foundation Fund, LLC.

Written and compiled by Rebecca Currington and Patricia Mitchell in association with Snapdragon Group℠, Tulsa, OK

Print ISBN 978-1-62029-163-4

eBook Editions:
Adobe Digital Edition (.epub) 978-1-62029-552-6
Kindle and MobiPocket Edition (.prc) 978-1-62029-551-9

Published by Barbour Publishing, Inc., P.O. Box 719, Uhrichsville, Ohio 44683,
www.barbourbooks.com

Our mission is to publish and distribute inspirational products offering exceptional value and biblical encouragement to the masses.

Member of the
Evangelical Christian
Publishers Association

Printed in China.

In the
Loving Father's
Care

Helen Steiner Rice

BARBOUR
PUBLISHING

Contents

God will redeem
me from the realm
of the dead;
he will surely take
me to himself.

PSALM 49:15 NIV

A New Reality

Our human minds have trouble processing the word *eternal*. In our world, everything has a beginning and an end; nothing goes on forever. The essence of eternity, however, is one of those new things we encounter when we come into fellowship with an eternal God. The finite nature of our lives is overruled—a new reality is set in place.

This new reality has so many implications. In fact, embracing the eternal changes everything. It gives us a future beyond the limitations of our physical bodies, and it gives us hope. Grief and loss are tempered by the understanding that death is only a momentary separation. We will be with our loved ones again, restored and more vibrant than ever.

Can you take hold of this new reality—eternal life? Let it sink in and realign your inner perspective. Then lift your face to God and smile!

Death Is the Gateway to Eternal Life

Death is just another step
  along life's changing way,
No more than just a gateway
  to a new and better day,
And parting from our loved ones
  is much easier to bear
When we know that they are waiting
  for us to join them there…
For it is on the wings of death
  that the living soul takes flight
Into the Promised Land of God
  where there shall be no night…

So death is just a natural thing,
   like the closing of a door
As we start up on a journey
   to a new and distant shore...
And none need make this journey
   undirected or alone,
For God promised us safe passage
   to this vast and great
   unknown...
So let your grief be softened
   and yield not to despair,
You have only placed your loved one
   in the loving Father's care.

—HSR

In Christ All Men
May Live Again

Let us all remember when
   our faith is running low,
Christ is more than just a figure
   wrapped in an ethereal glow.
For He came and dwelled among us
   and He knows our every need,
And He loves and understands us
   and forgives each sinful deed.
He was crucified and buried
   and rose again in glory,
And the Savior's resurrection
   makes the wondrous Easter story
An abiding reassurance
   that man dies to live again
In a land that's free from trouble
   where there's peace among all men.

—HSR

Living Forever

Eternal life. What does it really mean? Can we truly grasp the concept of living forever? And not only living, but living without the painful extremities of this present life.

The Bible tells us that there will be no more sadness or crying or disappointment or loss. There will be no discord or competition or greed. The joys of this life will be increased, while the sorrows will be gone forever. Pain and suffering will be banished and loneliness and isolation will be replaced by true fellowship. Hard to even imagine, isn't it? But that is what we've been promised. That is our heritage, our hope.

Ask God to help you see beyond the sadness of today to the joy of your future life with God. You may not fully understand the concept of eternal life until you are there, but the very thought of it will brighten your here and now.

Death Opens the Door
to Life Evermore

We live a short while on earth below,
Reluctant to die, for we do not know
Just what dark death is all about,
And so we view it with fear and doubt.
Not certain of what is around the bend,
We look on death as the final end
To all that made us mortal beings,
And yet there lies beyond our seeing
A beautiful life so full and complete
That we should leave with hurrying feet
To walk with God by sacred streams
Amid beauty and peace beyond our dreams,
For all who believe in the risen Lord
Have been assured of this reward,

And death for them is just graduation
To a higher realm of wide elevation.
For life on earth is a transient affair,
Just a few brief years in which to prepare
For a life that is free from pain and tears,
Where time is not counted by hours or years.
For death is only the method God chose
To colonize heaven with the souls of those
Who by their apprenticeship on earth
Proved worthy to dwell in the land
   of new birth.
So death is not sad, it's time for elation,
A joyous transition, the soul's emigration
Into a place where the soul's safe and free
To live with God through eternity.

—HSR

Our Father Will Provide

Death is a gateway our loved ones pass through
On their way to a land where we're all born anew,
And while we can't see what's on death's other side,
We know that our Father will richly provide
All that He promised to those who believe,
And His kingdom is waiting for us to receive.

—HSR

Prayer

"I called to the Lord
out of my distress,
and he answered me."

JONAH 2:2 NRSV

He Is Listening

There are times with all of us when we wonder where God has gone. We go headfirst into some frightening circumstance, and suddenly it seems like we've lost the sense of God's presence.

It's true that when we are overwhelmed emotionally, we sometimes grow numb, and that can make us feel alone, isolated, even abandoned. But it's important to remember during those times that regardless of how well we can or cannot feel His presence, God is there. He has promised never to leave us or forsake us, and He always keeps His word.

If you are feeling like God is out of reach, you need to know that He isn't. Open up to Him in prayer. Trust that, despite your feelings, He's by your side, right where He's always been, and He is listening, just as He promised.

God Will Not Fail You

When life seems empty
and there's no place to go,
When you heart is troubled
and your spirits are low,
When friends seem few
and nobody cares,
There is always God
to hear your prayers...
And whatever you're facing
will seem much less
When you go to God
and confide and confess,
For the burden that seems
too heavy to bear

God lifts away
   on the wings of prayer. . .
And seen through God's eyes
   earthly troubles diminish
And we're given new strength
   to face and to finish
Life's daily tasks
   as they come along
If we pray for strength
   to keep us strong. . .
So go to our Father
   when troubles assail you,
For His grace is sufficient
   and He'll never fail you.

                    —HSR

God's Stairway

Step by step we climb day by day
Closer to God with each prayer we pray,
For the cry of the heart offered in prayer
Becomes just another spiritual stair
In the heavenly place where we live anew...
So never give up, for it's worth the climb
To live forever in endless time
Where the soul of man is safe and free
To live and love through eternity.

–HSR

Tears in a Bottle

When our hearts are breaking, we sometimes feel frozen in place, words don't come easily—if at all. Have you ever felt that way? Though we may understand the need for prayer, we may also feel like it's quite impossible to express what we're going through, even to God.

God loves it when we come to Him, sincerely presenting our thoughts through our words. But for God, words aren't really necessary. He sees and hears the deepest cries of our hearts. The Bible says He hears every anguished groan and keeps our tears in a bottle.

In your darkest hour, reach out to God with your heart, and you will feel Him reach back with comfort and strength and peace. He is waiting, longing to answer your prayers regardless of how they come to Him. Trust Him, knowing that nothing is too big for our almighty heavenly Father.

On the Wings of Prayer

On the wings of prayer
  our burdens take flight
And our load of care
  becomes bearably light
And our heavy hearts
  are lifted above
To be healed by the balm
  of God's wonderful love...
And the tears in our eyes
  are dried by the hands
Of a loving Father
  who understands
All of our problems,
  our fears and despair
When we take them to Him
  on the wings of prayer.

—HSR

It's Me Again, God

Remember me, God?
　I come every day
Just to talk with You, Lord,
　and to learn how to pray.
You make me feel welcome,
　You reach out Your hand.
I need never explain,
　for You understand.
I come to You frightened
　and burdened with care,
So lonely and lost
　and so filled with despair,
And suddenly, Lord,
　I'm no longer afraid—
My burden is lighter
　and the dark shadows fade.
Oh, God, what a comfort
　to know that You care
And to know when I seek You,
　You will always be there.

—HSR

God, Are You There?

I'm way down here—You're way up there
Are You sure You can hear my faint,
   faltering prayer?
For I'm so unsure of just how to pray—
To tell You the truth, God, I don't know what to say.
I just know I'm lonely and vaguely disturbed,
Bewildered and restless, confused and perturbed,
And they tell me that prayer
   helps to quiet the mind
And to unburden the heart, for in stillness we find
A newborn assurance that someone does care
And someone does answer each small,
   sincere prayer.

—HSR

Peace

And God's peace,
which is so great we
cannot understand it....

PHILIPPIANS 4:7 NCV

Peace that Lasts

Nothing destroys peace as quickly as disappointment or loss. Our minds work overtime trying to imagine how things could have gone differently—all for nothing of course. That's because we often settle for a form of peace that is far too fragile. It's a simple peace of mind based on wish and conjecture.

The peace that God gives reigns over all our circumstances, both good and adverse. And it isn't based on the unstable nature of our human minds and emotions. Instead, peace that lasts is based on our faith and trust in almighty God. It comes from placing our lives confidently in His care.

If you have need of peace today, why bother with a flimsy peace that comes from hoping for the best. Ask God to give you His peace, a peace that rides above the storms of life and is there to comfort and calm you when you need it most.

The Peace of Meditation

So we may know God better
   and feel His quiet power,
Let us daily keep in silence
   a meditation hour...
For to understand God's greatness
   and to use His gifts each day,
The soul must learn to meet Him
   in a meditative way...
For our Father tells His children
   that if they would know His will
They must seek Him in the silence
   when all is calm and still...
For nature's great forces
   are found in quiet things
Like softly falling snowflakes
   drifting down on angels' wings

Or petals dropping soundlessly
from a lovely full-blown rose,
So God comes closest to us
when our souls are in repose...
So let us plan with prayerful care
to always allocate
A certain portion of each day
to be still and meditate...
For when everything is quiet
and we're lost in meditation,
Our souls are then preparing
for a deeper dedication
That will make it wholly possible
to quietly endure
The violent world around us,
for in God we are secure.

—HSR

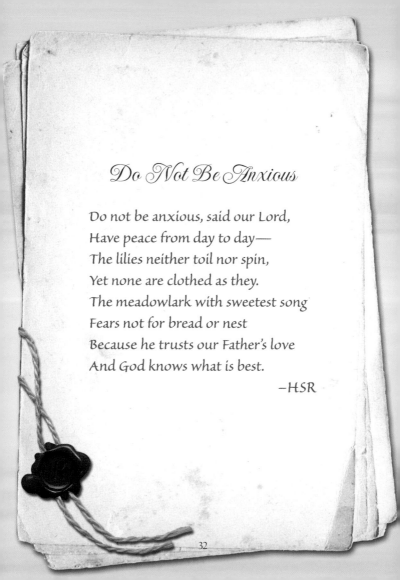

Do Not Be Anxious

Do not be anxious, said our Lord,
Have peace from day to day—
The lilies neither toil nor spin,
Yet none are clothed as they.
The meadowlark with sweetest song
Fears not for bread or nest
Because he trusts our Father's love
And God knows what is best.

                                    —HSR

True Peace

What is peace? Most people understand it to mean a state of calm and tranquility or freedom from troubling thoughts and emotions. Considering the world we live in and the frailties of our humanness, it could be argued that we have no chance at all for peace in this life. But fortunately, there is a form of peace that transcends the world around us and can even penetrate and disarm our troubled hearts and minds. It's the peace that comes from God Himself.

What makes this peace so powerful? Its source is not subject to life's extremities. Not only is God able to offer solace and encouragement, He also has the power to change our circumstances, or if He chooses, lift us up above them. He is able to make our circumstances work out for our good.

Don't look for peace in all the wrong places. Look to God, the source of true peace.

The Soul of Man

Every man has a deep heart need
That cannot be filled
  with doctrine or creed,
For the soul of man
  knows nothing more
Than just that he is longing for
A haven that is safe and sure,
A fortress where he feels secure,
An island in this sea of strife,
Away from all the storms of life.
Oh God of love, who sees us all,
You are so great—we are so small.
Hear man's universal prayer
Crying to You in despair,
"Save my soul and grant me peace,
Let my restless murmurings cease.

God of love, forgive, forgive.
Teach me how to truly live.
Ask me not my race or creed,
Just take me in my hour of need
And let me know You love me, too,
And that I am a part of You."
And someday may man realize
That all the earth, the seas, and skies
Belong to God, who made us all—
The rich, the poor, the great, the small—
And in the Father's holy sight
No man is yellow, black, or white. . .
And peace on earth cannot be found
Until we meet on common ground
And every man becomes a brother
Who worships God and loves each other.

—HSR

Peace Begins in the Home and the Heart

Peace is not something you fight for
   with bombs and missiles that kill—
Peace is attained in the silence
   that comes when the heart stands still. . .
For hearts that are restless and warlike
   with longings that never cease
Can never contribute ideas
   that bring the world nearer to peace. . .
For as dew never falls on a morning
   that follows a dark, stormy night,
The peace and grace of our Father
   fall not on a soul in flight. . .
So if we seek peace for all people, there is but one
      place to begin,
       And the armament race will not win it,
        for the fortress of peace is within.

                    −HSR

Renewal

Outwardly we are wasting away, yet inwardly we are being renewed day by day.
2 CORINTHIANS 4:16 NIV

All Things New

Have you ever felt that your life was in ruins? *Nothing will ever be the same*, you told yourself. We have all felt that way at one time or another, which is why it's so wonderful to be able to say that God can make all things new. There's a fresh start waiting no matter how badly we have messed up or lost out.

Life has a way of chalking up losses, but God has a way of taking those losses and making them into something worthwhile. God wants to put you back on the winning side, but He won't intervene in your life without your permission. You must invite Him to come in and make the best out of your worst.

Our God is a loving and gentle Father who wants only the best for His children. Offer Him the losses in your life. Ask Him to renew and restore you.

Spring Awakens What Autumn Puts to Sleep

A garden of asters in varying hues,
Crimson pinks and violet blues,
Blossoming in the hazy fall,
Wrapped in autumn's lazy pall...
But early frost stole in one night,
And like a chilling, killing blight
It touched each pretty aster's head,
And now the garden's
    still and dead,
And all the lovely
    flowers that bloomed
Will soon be buried and entombed
In winter's icy shroud of snow...
But oh, how wonderful to know

That after winter
   comes the spring
To breathe new life in everything,
And all the flowers
   that fell in death
Will be awakened
   by spring's breath...
For in God's plan
   both men and flowers
Can only reach bright,
   shining hours
By dying first to rise in glory
And prove again the Easter story.

                              —HSR

There's Always a Springtime

After the winter comes the spring
  to show us again that in everything
There's always a renewal
  divinely planned,
Flawlessly perfect, the work of God's hand.
And just like the seasons that come and go
When the flowers of spring
  lay buried in snow,
God sends to the heart
  in its winter of sadness
A springtime awakening
  of new hope and gladness,
And loved ones who sleep
  in a season of death
Will, too, be awakened
  by God's life-giving breath.

—HSR

Renew and Restore

When wildfire rushed through Yellowstone National Park, laying waste to all in its path, there was a national sigh of anguish. All that natural beauty lost. But a few years later, green slowly began to overrule the blackness—grass, flowers, new seedlings were popping up everywhere. Nature tells us that our God is a God of renewal and restoration. It is His custom to take our damaged lives and make them into something fresh and beautiful again.

You may have experienced a wildfire in your life that left you feeling hopeless and destroyed. If you have, you wonder if you will have to live with the blackness forever. You ask yourself if you will ever experience beauty again.

There is always hope for renewal and restoration with God. Take your life to Him, and ask Him to bring back the springtime and new growth. It's what He does best.

Renewal

When life has lost its luster
  and it's filled with dull routine,
When you long to run away from it,
  seeking pastures new and green,
Remember, no one runs away from life
  without finding when they do
That you can't escape the thoughts you think
  that are pressing down on you—
For though the scenery may be different,
  it's the same old heart and mind
And the same old restless longings
  that you tried to leave behind...
So when your heart is heavy
  and your day is dull with care,
Instead of trying to escape,
  why not withdraw in prayer?

For in prayer there is renewal
    of the spirit, mind, and heart,
For everything is lifted up
    in which God has a part—
For when we go to God in prayer,
    our thoughts are rearranged,
So even though our problems
    have not been solved or changed,
Somehow the good Lord gives us
    the power to understand
That He who holds tomorrow
    is the One who holds our hands.

                                    —HSR

Nothing Is Lost Forever

The waking earth in springtime
Reminds us it is true
That nothing ever really dies
That is not born anew...
So trust God's all wise wisdom
And doubt the Father never,
For in His heavenly kingdom
There is nothing lost forever.

—HSR

Comfort

The LORD wants to show his mercy to you. He wants to rise and comfort you.

ISAIAH 30:18 NCV

Always There

People mean well. They want to help when we experience sadness or loss and often they do— for a while. But as time goes on, people return to their own lives and interests, and they expect that we will do the same. That's just the reality of it.

But God isn't limited by our human realities. He is a friend who will stand by us long after the acceptable adjustment period is over. He's there for us day after day after day, helping us put the pieces of our world back together again. He's there helping us find joy and peace and courage to go on.

If you have experienced loss, let God comfort you as only He can, not just for one day, or two, but for every day of your life. He will never lose interest. He will always be there.

When Trouble Comes and Things Go Wrong

Let us go quietly to God
    when troubles come to us.
Let us never stop to whimper
    or complain or fret or fuss.
Let us hide our thorns in roses
    and our sighs in golden song
And let our crosses in a crown
    of smiles whenever things go
    wrong. . .
For no one can really help us
    as our troubles we bemoan,
For comfort, help, and inner peace
    must comes from God alone. . .
So do not tell your neighbor,
    your companion, or your friend

In the hope that they can help you
   bring your troubles to an end,
For they too have their problems—
   they are burdened just like you—
So take your cross to Jesus,
   and He will see you through. . .
And waste no time in crying
   on the shoulder of a friend,
But go directly to the Lord,
   for on Him you can depend. . .
For there's absolutely nothing
   that His mighty hand can't do,
And He never is too busy
   to help and comfort you.

                              —HSR

Only God

At times like these
Man is helpless...
It is only God
Who can speak the words
That calm the sea,
Still the wind,
And ease the pain...
So lean on Him
And you will never walk alone.

—HSR

He Understands

Some kinds of losses have to be experienced to be understood. Until then, our words may seem shallow, even trite. It isn't that we don't care, it's just that we don't have the passion that only comes from walking through similar heartaches and pain.

That's one thing we can be sure of when our heavenly Father comforts us. He knows how we feel because He's been there Himself. He experienced the loss of His Son, Jesus, on our behalf. He watched Him suffer. He knows how that feels.

You may be walking down roads you have never traveled before, paths strewn with heartache and suffering. God sees you, and He is reaching out to you right now. He knows what you're going through. Receive His comfort. Let Him help you pass through the valley of suffering, and one day you will be able to help others.

Before You Can Dry Another's Tears, You Too Must Weep

Let me not live a life that's free
From the things that draw me
  close to Thee,
For how can I ever hope to heal
The wounds of others I do not feel?
If my eyes are dry and I never weep,
How do I know when the hurt is deep?
If my heart is cold and it never bleeds,
How can I tell what my brother needs?
For when ears are deaf to the beggar's plea
And we close our eyes and refuse to see
And we steel our hearts
  and harden our minds
And we count it a weakness
  whenever we're kind,
We are no longer following
  the Father's way

Or seeking His guidance from day to day...
For without crosses to carry
   and burdens to bear,
We dance through a life
   that is frothy and fair,
And chasing the rainbow
   we have no desire
For roads that are rough
   and realms that are higher...
So spare me no heartache
   or sorrow, dear Lord,
For the heart that hurts
   reaps the richest reward,
And God blesses the heart
   that is broken with sorrow
As He opens the door
   to a brighter tomorrow...
For only through tears can we recognize
The suffering that lies in another's eyes.

                                   —HSR

When I Must Leave You

When I must leave you for a little while,
Please do not grieve and shed wild tears
And hug your sorrow to you through the years,
But start out bravely with a gallant smile.
Spend not your life in empty days,
But fill each waking hour in useful ways,
Reach out your hand in comfort and cheer,
And I in return will comfort you and hold you near.

—HSR

Blessing

The grace of our Lord Jesus
Christ be with your spirit.

PHILEMON 1:25 NCV

All Your Blessings

Do you count your blessings? All of them? Or just the happy, comfortable kind of blessing?

What about the coworker who is always challenging you? But wait. . .what if that person's annoying behavior is motivating you to do a better job and find greater success? Or how about the traffic backup that kept you sitting and waiting for forty-five minutes? What if that traffic snarl gave you forty-five minutes of uninterrupted conversation with your teenager? It's difficult to see the unpleasant circumstances in life as blessings, but without them we would miss so much.

What you're going through right now may have you down for the count. But even on your back looking up there are blessings to be had—the kindness of a friend, the comfort of your heavenly Father, time to rest, a new perspective. Think about it and then start counting *all* your blessings.

Blessings Devised by God

God speaks to us in many ways,
Altering our lives, our plans, and our days,
And His blessings come in many guises
That He alone in love devises,
And sorrow, which we dread so much,
Can bring a very healing touch...
For when we fail to heed His voice
We leave the Lord no other choice
Except to use a firm, stern hand
To make us know He's in command...

For on the wings of loss and pain,
The peace we often sought in vain
Will come to us with sweet surprise,
For God is merciful and wise...
And through dark hours of tribulation
God gives us time for meditation,
And nothing can be counted loss
Which teaches us to bear our cross.

—HSR

God's Keeping

To be in God's keeping is surely a blessing,
For though life is often dark and distressing,
No day is too dark and no burden too great
That God in His love cannot penetrate.

—HSR

The Littlest Blessings

What do you do when the sadness in your life is overwhelming, when it seems like you cannot, will not ever be happy again? When you're in that place, how do you begin to take back your joy, how do you open a hole in the sadness to let the sun shine down on you again?

When life seems impossible, focus on the littlest of blessings. Your four-year-old's giggle, your puppy's floppy ears, your favorite poem. Those wonderful little gifts that you usually take for granted. Those little blessings are the touchstones that will guide you through the fog of tears back to your life. Like small meals help you to recover after a bout of illness, little blessings are easier to take hold of, to rejoice in.

Whatever you are going through, count your littlest blessings. Let them remind you that you will be happy again one day. You really will!

Count Your Gains,
Not Losses

As we travel down life's busy road
Complaining of our heavy load,
We often think God's been unfair
And gave us much more than our share
Of daily little irritations
And disappointing tribulations.
We're discontented with our lot
And all the bad breaks that we got.
We count our losses not our gain,
And remember only tears and pain.
The good things we forget completely,
When God looked down
   and blessed us sweetly.
Our troubles fill our every thought,
We dwell upon the goals we sought,

And wrapped up in our own despair,
We have no time to see or share
Another's load that far outweighs
Our little problems and dismays. . .
And so we walk with heads held low,
And little do we guess or know
That someone near us on life's street
Is burdened deeply with defeat,
And if we'd but forget our care
And stop in sympathy to share
The burden that our brother carried,
Our minds and hearts would be less harried
And we would feel our load was small—
In fact, we carried no load at all.

–HSR

Blessings Come in Many Guises

When troubles come and things go wrong
And days are cheerless and nights are long,
We find it so easy to give in to despair
By magnifying the burdens we bear.
We add to our worries by refusing to try
To look for the rainbow in an overcast sky,
And the blessings God sent in a darkened disguise
Our troubled hearts fail to recognize,
Not knowing God sent it not to distress us
But to strengthen our faith
    and redeem us and bless us.

                                        —HSR

Strength

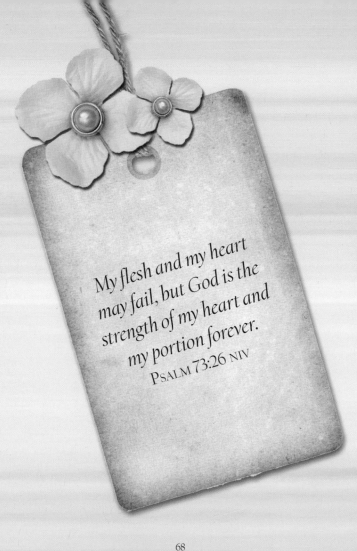

My flesh and my heart
may fail, but God is the
strength of my heart and
my portion forever.

PSALM 73:26 NIV

His Strength

Have you ever run into something or fallen and had the air knocked out of you? It's a strange feeling. Your body has sustained a shock, and it freezes up, leaving you feeling weak and powerless. A great loss in your life can leave you feeling the same way.

When God says in the Bible that He wants to give you His strength, He doesn't mean you will become more muscular because of His presence in your life. Instead He means that His strength will sustain you when you get the air knocked out of you, when you get thrown up against the wall by one of life's surprises.

No matter what circumstance has come into your life—sickness, bereavement, betrayal, to name just a few—reach out to God. Soon you will feel Him holding you, lifting you, strengthening you until you can breathe easily again.

The End of the Road
Is but a Bend in the Road

When we feel we have nothing left to give
    and we are sure that the song has ended,
When our day seems over and the shadows fall
    and the darkness of night has descended,
Where can we go to find the strength
    to valiantly keep on trying?
Where can we find the hand that will dry
    the tears that the heart is crying?
There's but one place to go and that is to God,
    and dropping all pretense and pride,
We can pour out our problems without restraint
    and gain strength with Him at our side...
And together we stand at life's crossroads
    and view what we think is the end,

But God has a much bigger vision,
   and He tells us it's only a bend...
For the road goes on and is smoother,
   and the pause in the song is a rest,
And the part that's unsung and unfinished
   is the sweetest and richest and best...
So rest and relax and grow stronger—
   let go and let God share your load.
Your work is not finished or ended—
   you've just come to a bend in the road.

—HSR

Dark Shadows Fall
in the Lives of Us All

Sickness and sorrow come to us all,
But through it we grow and learn to stand tall,
For trouble is part and parcel of life,
And no man can grow without struggle and strife.
The more we endure with patience and grace,
The stronger we grow and the more we can face,
And the more we can face, the greater our love,
And with love in our hearts
   we are more conscious of
The pain and the sorrow in lives everywhere,
So it is through trouble that we learn to share.

—HSR

The Source of Strength

If you've ever been sick, you know that even after you're well again, it takes awhile for your strength to be restored. Your body has called on all your strength and resources to heal itself, and now those resources have to be replenished. The same is true when you experience an emotional injury, like a deep disappointment or loss.

Since God is the source of all things, He is able to help you through whatever crisis has left you emotionally drained. In fact, the Bible says that when you are at your weakest point, God is there to infuse you with His strength.

You need never suffer alone. God loves you and cares about you more than you can even imagine. He's standing by to comfort and strengthen you, but He won't push His way into your life. He waits for you to ask. Won't you reach out to Him?

A Word of Understanding

May peace and understanding
Give you strength and courage, too,
And may the hours and days ahead
Hold a new hope for you;
For the sorrow that is yours today
Will pass away and then
You'll find the sun of happiness
Will shine for you again.

—HSR

In God Is My Strength

"Love divine, all loves excelling,"
   make my humbled heart your dwelling...
For without Your love divine,
   total darkness would be mine.
My earthly load I could not bear
   if You were not there to share
All the pain, despair, and sorrow
   that almost make me dread tomorrow,
For I am often weak and weary,
   and life is dark and bleak and dreary...
But somehow when I realize
   that He who made the sea and skies
And holds the whole world in His hand
   has my small soul in His command,
It gives me strength to try once more
   to somehow reach the heavenly door
Where I will live forevermore
   with friends and loved ones I adore.

—HSR

Why Am I Complaining?

My cross is not too heavy, my road is not too rough
Because God walks beside me,
 and to know this is enough...
And though I get so lonely, I know I'm not alone,
For the Lord God is my Father
 and He loves me as His own...
So though I'm tired and weary
 and I wish my race were run,
God will only terminate it
 when my work on earth is done...
So let me stop complaining about my load of care,
For God will always lighten it
 when it gets too much to bear...

   And if He does not ease my load,
    He'll give me strength to bear it,
   For God, in love and mercy,
    is always near to share it.

                              —HSR

Faith

Through [Christ] you
believe in God, who raised
him from the dead and
glorified him, and so your
faith and hope are in God.

1 PETER 1:21 NIV

An Oasis of Certainty

How will things turn out? It's a question we ask ourselves over and over again when anxiety steals our rest. We long to know what tomorrow has in store, and our spirits thirst for certainty.

In the midst of your worries, God reaches out to you. He leans down to you, bidding you to place your troubles in His hands and rest your head on His shoulders. After you have poured out everything that burdens your heart, He moves to enliven, deepen, and strengthen your faith in Him. He cleanses you in the cooling waters of His sure and certain promise to be with you always, no matter what the days and years may bring.

Breathe deeply and rest easily in the assurance of His love. Let Him fill you with the serenity only faith can bring. Come to the oasis of God's compassion and care.

Faith for Dark Days

When dark days come—
 and they come to us all—
We feel so helpless and lost and small.
We cannot fathom the reason why,
And it is futile for us to try
To find the answer, the reason or cause,
For the master plan is without any flaws. . .
And when the darkness
 shuts out the light,
We must lean on faith to restore our sight,

For there is nothing we need know
If we have faith that wherever we go
God will be there to help us to bear
Our disappointments, pain, and care,
For He is our shepherd,
  our Father, our Guide,
And you're never alone
  with the Lord at your side...
So may the Great Physician attend you,
And may His healing completely mend you.

                              −HSR

Let Go and Let God

When you're troubled and worried
  and sick at heart
And your plans are upset
  and your world falls apart,
Remember God's ready and waiting to share
The burden you find too heavy to bear. . .
So with faith, let go and let God lead the way
Into a brighter and less-troubled day.
For God has a plan for everyone,
If we learn to pray, "Thy will be done."
For nothing in life is without God's design
For each life is fashioned
  by the hand that's divine.

—HSR

The Father's Arms

On the playground, a young boy scampers up the tall ladder of a shiny new slide. Once at the top where he can see down its steep slope, however, his face freezes in fear. Terrified, he begins to sob.

Then his father appears at the bottom of the slide. He calls his son's name, holds out his arms, and invites the boy to come. The boy dries his tears, bravely releases himself, and then whizzes down right into his father's waiting arms.

Faith in your heavenly Father's waiting arms gives you the assurance to face the changes and challenges ahead of you. Even if you should stumble along the way, your Father's arms will catch you and help you stand up again. Listen for your name and God's words of encouragement to you. Put your faith in His strength, never fearing that He will let you fall.

We Can't, But God Can

Why things happen as they do
  we do not always know,
And we cannot always fathom
  why our spirits sink so low.
We flounder in our dark distress,
  we are wavering and unstable,
But when we're most inadequate,
  the Lord God's always able—
For though we are incapable,
  God's powerful and great,
And there's no darkness of the mind
  God cannot penetrate...
And all that is required of us
  whenever things go wrong
Is to trust in God implicitly
  with a faith that's deep and strong...

And while He may not instantly
  unravel all the strands
Of the tangled thoughts that trouble us,
  He completely understands—
And in His time, if we have faith,
  He will gradually restore
The brightness to our spirits
  that we've been longing for...
So remember there's no cloud too dark
  for God's light to penetrate
If we keep on believing
  and have faith enough to wait.

                                        —HSR

You Are Never Alone

There's truly nothing we need know
If we have faith wherever we go,
God will be there to help us bear
Our disappointments, pain, and care,
For He is our shepherd, our Father, our Guide,
You're never alone with the Lord at your side.

—HSR

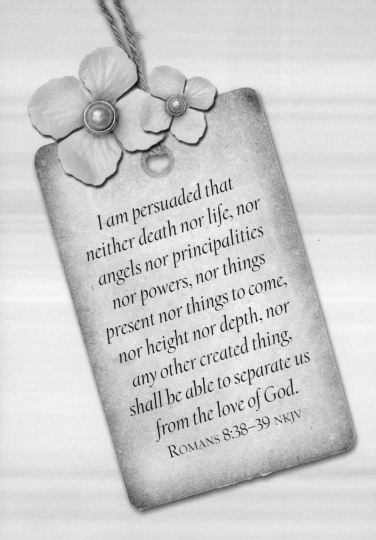

I am persuaded that
neither death nor life, nor
angels nor principalities
nor powers, nor things
present nor things to come,
nor height nor depth, nor
any other created thing,
shall be able to separate us
from the love of God.

ROMANS 8:38–39 NKJV

Loving Yourself

Do you love yourself? Out of humility, you might be tempted to hedge that question. You recall your shortcomings and those things about yourself you would like to change or make better. Yet despite anything in your past or your present, God invites you to love yourself with the same unwavering conviction and commitment with which He loves you.

Even before you were born, God showed His love for you by sending His Son into the world to bring you into relationship with Him. Jesus' sacrificial death tells you how much God values you, and His resurrection from the dead demonstrates God's desire to bring you to eternal life with Him. There's nothing about you that could alter His love, and everything about you to love.

Again, do you love yourself? Let your answer rest confidently in His overflowing and unchanging love for you.

Where There Is Love

Where there is love the heart is light,
Where there is love the day is bright.
Where there is love there is a song
To help when things are going wrong.
Where there is love there is a smile
To make all things seem more
   worthwhile.
Where there is love there's a quiet peace,
A tranquil place where turmoils cease.
Love changes darkness into light
And makes the heart take wingless flight.

Oh, blessed are those who walk in love,
They also walk with God above...
And when you walk with God each day
And kneel together when you pray,
Your marriage will be truly blessed
And God will be your daily guest,
And love that once seemed yours alone
God gently blends into His own.

—HSR

Somebody Loves You

Somebody loves you more than you know,
Somebody goes with you wherever you go,
Somebody really and truly cares
And lovingly listens to all of your prayers. . .
Don't doubt for a minute that this is not true,
For God loves His children
    and takes care of them, too. . .
And all of His treasures are yours to share
If you love Him completely
    and show that you care. . .
And if you walk in His footsteps
    and have faith to believe,
There's nothing you ask for
    that you will not receive!

                                            –HSR

Loving the Unlovable

Some people aren't easy to love. They're the ones whose words and actions grate and irritate, and even harm others. Though we would like to put distance between ourselves and them, they're the ones most in need of our closeness and caring.

God extends His love to everyone, and He bids us to follow His example. In one way, His command presents an impossible task! Yet in another way, it invites assurance and comfort, for God loves us, even when we're at our most unlovable. Nothing we can do could make Him reconsider His love or withhold His forgiveness when we turn to Him. Our acceptance of His love enables us to take on the "impossible" task of loving others.

The person you find hardest to love may be the person most in need of your love and heartfelt prayers.

God's Love Is a Haven in the Storms of Life

God's love is like an island
  in life's ocean vast and wide,
A peaceful, quiet shelter
  from the restless, rising tide.
God's love is like a fortress,
  and we seek protection there
When the waves of tribulation
  seem to drown us in despair.
God's love is a sanctuary
  where our souls can find sweet rest
From the struggle and the tension
  of life's fast and futile quest.

God's love is like a tower
   rising far above the crowd,
And God's smile is like the sunshine
   breaking through the threatening cloud.
God's love is like a beacon
   burning bright with faith and prayer,
And through all the changing scenes of life
   we can find a haven there.
For God's love is fashioned
   after something enduring called love
And it is endless and unfailing
   like His character above.

                    –HSR

Life

A little laughter, a little song,
A little teardrop
When things go wrong,
A little calm
And a little strife
A little loving—
And that is life.

                              —HSR

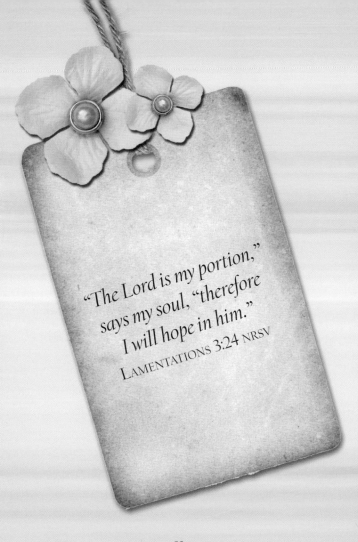

"The Lord is my portion,"
says my soul, "therefore
I will hope in him."
LAMENTATIONS 3:24 NRSV

A New Perspective

From a human perspective, there's no hope. The wounds are too deep, the damage too extensive; the patient has no chance of recovery. As we grieve in the darkness of trying times, God's strength and His presence light our way with what we need the most: life-giving, life-changing hope.

Jesus' resurrection from the grave affirms God's power over all forces, even death. From an act His enemies believed would end all hope of life, Jesus brought a new beginning. In the resurrected Christ, you have been delivered from the finality of death. In Him, your perspective changes. Through Him, you can see that the tomb is not the end, but the beginning.

When it looks to you as if there's no hope, go to Him. Pray for the spiritual vision to see beyond the grave to the sure and certain hope you have in life eternal.

Each Spring God Renews His Promise

Long, long ago in a land far away,
There came the dawn of the first Easter day,
And each year we see the promise reborn
That God gave the world
   on that first Easter morn.
For in each waking flower
   and each singing bird
The promise of Easter is witnessed and heard,
And spring is God's way of speaking to men
And renewing the promise of Easter again...

For death is a season
   that man must pass through,
And just like the flowers,
   God wakens him, too,
So why should we grieve
   when our loved ones die,
For we'll meet them again in a cloudless sky.
For Easter is more than a beautiful story—
It's the promise of life and eternal glory.

                         –HSR

A Message of Consolation

On the wings of death and sorrow
God sends us new hope for tomorrow,
And in His mercy and His grace
He gives us strength to bravely face
The lonely days that stretch ahead
And to know our loved one is not dead
But only sleeping out of our sight,
And we'll meet in that land
   where there is no night.

                                                                   —HSR

A Well-Founded Hope

In the middle of winter, when snow covers the ground and chill winds whip through barren trees, few signs of life remain. The songbirds have disappeared, the flowers have wilted, and leaden clouds hang low in the sky.

Yet you know that beneath the snow lie the seeds of spring. You can picture in your mind's eye the first green shoots that will peek up in the melting snow, and you can look forward to, once again, the fragrance of newly opened blossoms and the chattering of birds in the boughs of green, leafy trees.

Just as God turns the bleakness of winter to the gladness of spring, so He transforms sadness to joy, adversity to peace. This is your well-founded hope, and it's a hope as sure as winter turns to spring.

On the Other Side of Death

Death is a gateway
   we all must pass through
To reach that fair land
   where the soul's born anew,
For man's born to die,
   and his sojourn on earth
Is a short span of years
   beginning with birth.
And like pilgrims we wander
   until Death takes our hand
And we start on the journey
   to God's Promised Land,

A place where we'll find
   no suffering or tears,
Where time is not counted
   in days, months, or years.
And in that fair city that God has prepared
Are unending joys to be happily shared
With all of our loved ones
   who patiently wait
On death's other side to open the gate.

                                        —HSR

The Home Beyond

We feel so sad when those we love
Are called to live in the home above,
But why should we grieve when they say good-bye
And go to dwell in a cloudless sky?
For they have but gone to prepare the way,
And we'll meet them again some happy day,
For God has told us that nothing can sever
A life He created to live forever.
So let God's promise soften our sorrow
And give us new strength for a brighter tomorrow.

                                        —HSR

Joy

"Do not grieve,
for the joy of the
LORD is your strength."
NEHEMIAH 8:10 NIV

Yesterday, Today, and Always

No one rests untouched by hardship. Not one of us is immune to disaster or disappointment or loss. Yet God, who knows all things past, present, and future, gives us every reason to live joyfully.

For all the yesterdays God has seen us through, joyful thanksgiving enlivens our spirits. For His help and guidance today, a joyful confidence and courage is ours, banishing our fears. For His promise of love forever, joyful optimism enlightens our hearts and brings us peace of mind. This is the reason for our joy, even as we pass through a world beset with pain. And our joy is what touches others as we help, encourage, and comfort them with the message of God's ever-present love.

God has blessed you with joy, and His joy is with you always. Now that's something to feel good about!

What Is Life?

Life is a sojourn here on earth
Which begins the day God gives us birth.
We enter this world from the great unknown,
And God gives each spirit a form of its own
And endows this form with a heart and a soul
To spur man on to his ultimate goal...
And through the senses of feeling and seeing,
God makes man into a human being
So he may experience a mortal life
And through this period of smiles and strife
Prepare himself to return as he came,
For birth and death are in essence the same,

For both are fashioned by God's mighty hand,
And while we cannot understand,
We know we are born to die and arise,
For beyond this world in beauty lies
The purpose of living and the ultimate goal
God gives at birth to each seeking soul. . .
So enjoy your sojourn on earth and be glad
That God gives you a choice
 between good things and bad,
And only be sure that you heed God's voice
Whenever life asks you to make a choice.

—HSR

Be Glad

Be glad that your life has been full and complete,
Be glad that you've tasted the bitter and sweet.
Be glad that you've walked in sunshine and rain,
Be glad that you've felt both pleasure and pain.
Be glad that you've had such a full, happy life,
Be glad for your joy as well as your strife.
Be glad that you've walked with courage each day,
Be glad you've had strength for each step of the way.
Be glad for the comfort that you've found in prayer.
Be glad for God's blessings, His love, and His care.

–HSR

Showers of Joy

Have you ever resolved to find more joy in life? If you're like most of us, your determination soon turns to disappointment. Despite your strongest efforts to stay positive and upbeat, the inevitable pain and losses of life leave you with little to celebrate.

That's why God invites you to let Him shower you with His joy. He's willing and able to fill your heart with genuine, long-lasting joy—the joy of knowing that you belong to Him. God has the desire and power to awaken in you a spirit of awe and appreciation, contentment and peace. Because God delights in you, He delights to bless you every day with life's simple wonders, pleasures, and joys.

Today, relax and let your joyous and joy-giving God do the work He is so good at. You won't be disappointed.

Expectation! Anticipation! Realization!

God gives us a power
  we so seldom employ
For we're so unaware
  it is filled with such joy.
The gift that God gives us is anticipation,
Which we can fulfill
  with sincere expectation,
For there's power in belief
  when we think we will find
Joy for the heart and peace for the mind,

And believing the day
    will bring a surprise
Is not only pleasant
    but surprisingly wise...
For we open the door
    to let joy walk through
When we learn to expect
    the best and the most, too,
And believing we'll find a happy surprise
Makes reality out of a fancied surmise.

                                              —HSR

Never Borrow
Sorrow from Tomorrow

Deal only with the present—
   never step into tomorrow,
For God asks us just to trust Him
   and to never borrow sorrow,
For the future is not ours to know,
   and it may never be,
So let us live and give our best and give it lavishly. . .
For to meet tomorrow's troubles
   before they are even ours
Is to anticipate the Savior
   and to doubt His all-wise powers,
So let us be content
      to solve our problems one by one,
      Asking nothing of tomorrow
         except "Thy will be done."

—HSR

God is so good, and by raising Jesus from death, he has given us new life and a hope that lives on.

1 PETER 1:3 CEV

New Has Come

Not all of life's changes are welcome. Some bring disappointment or heartache; many cause anxiety or sorrow. Yet, with God's help, we get through them and most often emerge wiser, more mature, and with a deepened understanding of ourselves.

Later, when looking back, we frequently realize that something more has come from the change we had to undergo. Perhaps it took us to another place, where happiness awaited us; or opened an unexpected opportunity to learn and do new things; or brought special people into our lives, people who continue to enrich our days with their caring and friendship.

A difficult change, while the ending of one thing, marks the beginning of something new. Let the excitement of the new help you lay down the old and move on. Ask for God's help and guidance through the changes you're facing today.

Life Is Forever!
Death Is a Dream!

If we did not go to sleep at night,
We'd never awaken to see the light,
And the joy of watching a new day break
Or meeting the dawn by some quiet lake
Would never be ours unless we slept
While God and all His angels kept
A vigil through this little death
That's over with the morning's breath...

And death, too, is a time of sleeping,
For those who die are in God's keeping,
And there's a sunrise for each soul,
For life, not death, is God's promised goal. . .
So trust God's promise and doubt Him never,
For only through death can man live forever.

—HSR

The Blessed Assurance of Easter

Easter means beauty and new life and spring.
It means the awakening of each sleeping thing,
And in that awakening the world sees again
The promise of life God gave to all men...
For God sent His Son to bless and to save
And redeem us from sin and death and the grave.

–HSR

A New Person

When you say you feel like a new person, it might be because you've improved your health through diet and exercise. Or maybe you've made another much-needed change in your life. But when God works in you, you don't simply feel like a new person. You *are* a new person!

God enters your heart to bring about real and lasting change. He infuses your heart with a new attitude of patience, compassion, and hope. He banishes fear, mends your broken places, and nurtures confident faith. Through His life-giving Spirit, He lifts from you the burden of guilt and cleanses you in the pure waters of His forgiveness. Every day, He restores and refreshes you as you grow in love for Him and for others.

Your relationship with God has made you a new person. It shows in the things you do and say, and in the way you live your life for Him.

The Soul, Like Nature, Has Seasons, Too

When you feel cast down
  and despondently sad
And you long to be happy
  and carefree and glad,
Do you ask yourself, as I so often do,
Why must there be days
  that are cheerless and blue?
Why is the song silenced
  in the heart that was gay?
And then I ask God what makes life this way,
And His explanation
  makes everything clear—
The soul has its seasons the same as the year.
Man, too, must pass through
  life's autumn of death
And have his heart frozen
  by winter's cold breath,

But spring always comes
  with new life and birth,
Followed by summer to warm the soft earth...
And oh, what a comfort
  to know there are reasons
That souls, like nature,
  must too have their seasons—
Bounteous seasons and barren ones, too,
Times for rejoicing and times to be blue...
For with nothing but sameness
  how dull life would be,
For only life's challenge can set the soul free...
And it takes a mixture
  of both bitter and sweet
To season our lives and make them complete.

                                     —HSR

This Too Will Pass Away

If I can endure for this minute
   whatever is happening to me
No matter how heavy my heart is
   or how dark the moment might be—
If I can remain calm and quiet
   with all my world crashing about me,
Secure in the knowledge God loves me
   when everyone else seems to doubt me—
If I can but keep on believing
   what I know in my heart to be true,
That darkness will fade with the morning
   and that this will pass away, too—
Then nothing in life can defeat me,
   for as long as this knowledge remains,
I can suffer whatever is happening,
   for I know God will break all the chains
That are binding me tight in the
          darkness and trying to fill me
          with fear. . .
        For there is no night without
          dawning, and I know that my
          morning is near.

                        –HSR

God loved us, and through
his grace he gave us a good
hope and encouragement
that continues forever.

2 Thessalonians 2:17 NCV

An Encouraging Word

Occasionally, everyone needs encouragement.
No doubt you remember when you were
suffering and someone said just the right thing.
It provided comfort and confidence. While
God often sends encouragement to you through
the words of others, He also encourages you
through His Spirit at work in you.

When you put your doubts and misgivings
into His hands, you make room for His
reassuring promises to strengthen your heart
and mind. Knowing you are relying on His
power, and not on your own, gives you the boost
you need to get through a difficult situation.
Believing in His unconditional love for you lifts
you from the depths of fear to the heights
of courage and fortitude.

Like nothing else, God's presence in
all life's circumstances is an unfailing
source of encouragement and help.
Call on Him wherever you are.
He's there for you.

In Hours of Discouragement, God Is Our Encouragement

Sometimes we feel uncertain
   and unsure of everything,
Afraid to make decisions,
   dreading what the day will bring.
We keep wishing it were possible
   to dispel all fear and doubt
And to understand more readily
   just what life is all about.
God has given us the answers,
   which too often go unheeded,
But if we search His promises
   we'll find everything that's needed
To lift our faltering spirits
   and renew our courage, too,

For there's absolutely nothing
　　too much for God to do...
For the Lord is our salvation
　　and our strength in every fight,
Our redeemer and protector,
　　our eternal guiding light.
He has promised to sustain us,
　　He's our refuge from all harms,
And underneath this refuge
　　are the everlasting arms...
So cast your burden on Him,
　　seek His counsel when distressed,
And go to Him for comfort
　　when you're lonely and oppressed...
For in God is our encouragement
　　in trouble and in trials,
And in suffering and in sorrow
　　He will turn our tears to smiles.

—HSR

An Easter Meditation

In the glorious Easter story,
   a troubled world can find
Blessed reassurance and
   enduring peace of mind...
For though we grow discouraged
   with this world we're living in,
There is comfort just in knowing
   God has triumphed over sin...
For our Savior's resurrection
   was God's way of telling men
That in Christ we are eternal
   and in Him we live again...
And to know life is unending
   and God's love is endless, too,
Makes our daily tasks and burdens
   so much easier to do...
And our earthly trials and troubles
   are but guideposts on the way
To the love and life eternal
   that God promises Easter day.

                          –HSR

Encouragement in Action

We encourage one another, often without realizing it. Sure, we know that sincere compliments, a hearty pat on the back, and words of genuine thanks and appreciation serve to encourage others. But we inspire them and support their efforts in many other ways as well.

When people see you react to heartache with determination and fortitude, they're apt to follow your example as they confront their own challenges. As you respond to others with kindness, thoughtfulness, and gentleness, you motivate many to "pass it on" to their family and friends. Your patience inspires patience, and your joy and faith prompt even more joy and faith in the world around you.

In times of loss, disappointment, and fear of failure, we all yearn for and need a little encouragement. Who could use your words, actions, example, and prayers today?

Give Me the Contentment
of Acceptance

In the deep, dark hours of my distress,
My unworthy life seems a miserable mess.
Handicapped, limited, with my strength decreasing,
The demands on my time keep forever increasing,
And I pray for the flair and the force of youth
So I can keep spreading God's light and His truth,
For my heart's happy hope and my dearest desire
Is to continue to serve You with fervor and fire,
But I no longer have strength to dramatically do
The spectacular things I loved doing for You.
Forgetting entirely that all You required
Was not a servant the world admired
But a humbled heart and a sanctified soul
Whose only mission and purpose and goal

Was to be content with whatever God sends
And to know that to please You really depends
Not on continued and mounting success
But on learning how to become less and less
And to realize that we serve God best
When our one desire and only request
Is not to succumb to worldly acclaim
But to honor ourselves in Your holy name.
So let me say no to the flattery and praise
And quietly spend the rest of my days
Far from the greed and the speed of man,
Who has so distorted God's simple life plan,
And let me be great in the eyes of You, Lord,
For that is the richest, most priceless reward.

—HSR

Never Be Discouraged

There is really nothing we need know
   or even try to understand
If we refuse to be discouraged
   and trust God's guiding hand,
So take heart and meet each minute
   with faith in God's great love,
Aware that every day of life
   is controlled by God above
And never dread tomorrow
   or what the future brings
Just pray for strength and courage
   and trust God in all things,
         And never grow discouraged—
          be patient and just wait,
         For God never comes too early,
          and He never comes too late.

                    —HSR

Rest

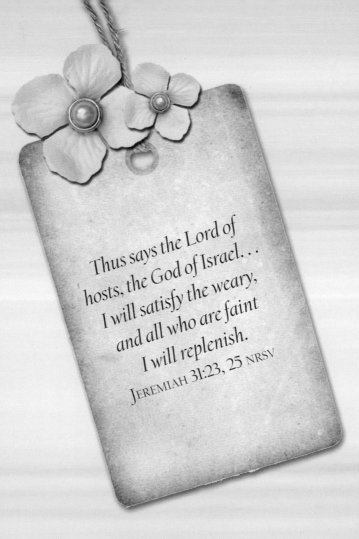

Thus says the Lord of
hosts, the God of Israel. . .
I will satisfy the weary,
and all who are faint
I will replenish.

JEREMIAH 31:23, 25 NRSV

Rest for the Weary

Doesn't a long, restful, and relaxing vacation sound nice right now? It isn't always possible to get away, however, even though you're exhausted by the demands of your work and responsibilities.

God's rest involves no packing or travel, no days away or dent in your wallet. Instead, God invites you to give Him the heavy burdens of your heart. That is, those worries that keep you from getting the sleep you need at night, and those wounds and resentments that shadow your outlook even on the sunniest days. With those things gone, you have the freedom to relax, truly relax, in the comfort of knowing He is there to guard and protect you, to help and defend you.

For a real vacation, rest at ease in God. It's one you can take right now, right where you are.

Anxious Prayers

When we are deeply disturbed by a problem
   and our minds are filled with doubt,
And we struggle to find a solution
   but there seems to be no way out,
We futilely keep on trying
   to untangle our web of distress,
but our own little, puny efforts
   meet with very little success.
And finally, exhausted and weary,
   discouraged and downcast and low,
With no foreseeable answer
   and with no other place to go,
We kneel down in sheer desperation
   and slowly and stumblingly pray,
then impatiently wait for an answer
   in one sudden instant, we say,

"God does not seem to be listening,
   so why should we bother to pray?"
But God can't get through to the anxious,
   who are much too impatient to wait,
You have to believe in God's promise
   that He comes not too soon or too late,
For whether God answers promptly
   or delays in answering your prayer,
you must have faith to believe Him
   and to know in your heart He'll be there.
So be not impatient or hasty,
   just trust in the Lord and believe,
For whatever you ask in faith and love,
   in abundance you are sure to receive.

                                        –HSR

This Is Just a Resting Place

Sometimes the road of life seems long
    as we travel through the years
And with hearts that are broken
    and eyes brimful of tears,
We falter in our weariness
    and sink beside the way,
But God leans down and whispers,
    "Child, there'll be another day,"
And the road will grow much smoother
    and much easier to face,
So do not be disheartened,
    this is just a resting place.

                                                   –HSR

You Have a Friend

There's something restful about talking with a true friend. You can say what's on your mind without fear of being criticized, and you can share your confidences with someone you trust.

Prayer is a conversation with God, your true and forever friend. He always has time for you, and there's nothing you could say that would change His love for you. You can relax in His presence, because He's interested in hearing you tell Him about all the events of your day, from the biggest to the smallest. He's not there to load you down with dos and don'ts, but to gently lead and guide you along His way.

When you pray, imagine God's look of empathy, His smile of understanding, and His touch of encouragement. Relax in His presence as if you were with the most wonderful friend you could ever have, because that's what He is.

The Seasons of the Soul

Why am I cast down and despondently sad
When I long to be happy and joyous and glad?
Why is my heart heavy with unbearable weight
As I try to escape this soul-saddened state?
I ask myself often what makes life this way,
Why is the song silenced in my heart today?
And then with God's help
   it all becomes clear—
The soul has its seasons
   just the same as the year.

I, too, must pass through life's autumn of dying,
A desolate period of heart-hurt and crying,
Followed by winter, in whose frostbitten hand
My heart is as frozen
    as the snow-covered land.
We, too, must pass through
    the seasons God sends,
Content in the knowledge
    that everything ends.

                                        −HSR

Life's Crossroads

Sometimes we come to life's crossroads
  and view what we think is the end,
But God has a much wider vision,
  and He knows it's only a bend,
The road will go on and get smoother,
  and after we've stopped for a rest,
The path that lies hidden beyond us
  is often the part that is best...
So rest and relax and grow stronger,
  let go and let God share your load,
And have faith in a brighter tomorrow,
  you've just come to a bend in the road.

—HSR

The fruit of that
righteousness will
be peace; its effect will
be quietness and
confidence forever.

ISAIAH 32:17 NIV

Peace and Quiet

We live in a noisy world—the sound of life in progress constantly booming around us. It fills shops and offices, and often our own homes. Wouldn't it be nice to escape to a place of peace and quiet?

This is particularly true when various circumstances in your life have left you feeling weak and confused. Recovery may depend on you being able to get away from the chaos long enough to let God's peace and calm wash over you. Even if you aren't the kind of person who typically appreciates solitude, you may find that time apart with God is the prescription for healing and wholeness.

Give yourself a much-needed break. Step away from the noise and into the welcoming arms of your compassionate Savior and Lord. In His presence you will find what you need. In His presence you will receive a new lease on life.

Not to Seek, Lord, but to Share

Dear God, much too often
  we seek You in prayer
Because we are wallowing
  in our own self-despair.
We make every word
  we lamentingly speak
An imperative plea for whatever we seek.
We pray for ourselves
  and so seldom for others—
We're concerned with our problems
  and not with our brothers.
We seem to forget, Lord,
  that the sweet hour of prayer
Is not for self-seeking
  but to place in Your care

All the lost souls, unloved and unknown,
And to keep praying for them
   until they're your own.
For it's never enough to seek God in prayer
With no thought of others
   who are lost in despair.
So teach us, dear God,
   that the power of prayer
Is made stronger by placing
   the world in Your care.

                              –HSR

Let Not Your
Heart Be Troubled

Whenever I am troubled
   and lost in deep despair,
I bundle all my troubles up
   and go to God in prayer. . .
I tell Him I am heartsick
   and lost and lonely, too,
That my mind is deeply burdened
   and I don't know what to do. . .
But I know He stilled the tempest
   and calmed the angry sea,
And I humbly ask if, in His love,
   He'll do the same for me. . .
And then I just keep quiet
   and think only thoughts of peace,
And if I abide in stillness
   my restless murmurings cease.

                       –HSR

A Place for You

When two people are in love with each other, they want to find a place of solitude and quietness. There they can be together, savor each other's company, and share the secrets of the heart.

In the same way, God's love for you draws Him close to you. He desires to come into the privacy of your heart and fill you with the tranquility and joy love craves. He invites you to speak about those things you may not have had the courage to tell another living soul. When there are no more words, or the feelings are too deep to express, love knows and understands. God's calm and gentle love embraces your soul in quietude and peace.

God, the one who loves you, stands at the door of your heart. He has come to the place where love has drawn Him, and now He knocks, desiring to enter in.

The Mystery of Prayer

Beyond that which words can interpret
   or theology explain,
The soul feels a shower of refreshment
   that falls like the gentle rain
On hearts that are parched with problems
   and are searching to find the way
To somehow attract God's attention
   through well-chosen words as they pray,
Not knowing that God in His wisdom
   can sense all man's worry and woe,
For there is nothing man can conceal
   that God does not already know...
So kneel in prayer in His presence
   and you'll find no need to speak,
For softly in quiet communion,
   God grants you the peace that you seek.

                                        —HSR

Listen in the Quietness

To try to run away from life is impossible to do,
For no matter where you chance to go,
  your troubles will follow you—
For though the scenery is different,
  when you look deep inside you'll find
The same deep, restless longings
  that you thought you left behind...
So when life becomes a problem
  much too great for us to bear,
Instead of trying to escape,
  let us withdraw in prayer—
For withdrawal means renewal
  if we withdraw to pray
And listen in the quietness to hear
  what God will say.

                              —HSR

Listen in Silence If You Would Hear

Silently the green leaves grow,
In silence falls the soft, white snow,
Silently the flowers bloom,
In silence sunshine fills a room—
Silently bright stars appear,
In silence velvet night draws near,
And silently God enters in
To free a troubled heart from sin...
For God works silently in lives.

—HSR

"Remember, I am
with you always,
to the end of the age."
MATTHEW 28:20 NRSV

The Garden of Your Heart

Picture a lovely garden. Yes, there are thistles here and there, and a few weeds have found their way in. But these aren't what catch your eye. Instead, you see an abundance of colorful blossoms and tender shoots. You delight in lush evergreens, flourishing vines, and fragrant flowers. The beauty of this garden moves your soul to thank God for the many splendors of His creation.

Like a garden, all life's seasons hold some sorrows, but many more joys. Both briers of pain and blossoms of happiness grow together, sometimes side by side; but happiness is brighter and much more delightful to look at.

Today, your heart may be aching, you may feel like your garden is cold and dead. If that's so, remind yourself of winters past. No matter how long the winter occupies your garden, spring always comes at last. One day soon, your garden will be beautiful again.

When My Soul at Last Finds Peace

Today my soul is reaching out
   for something that's unknown.
I cannot grasp or fathom it,
   for it's known to God alone.
I cannot hold or harness it
   or put it into form,
For it's as uncontrollable
   as the wind before the storm.
I know not where it came from
   or whither it will go.
For it's as inexplicable
   as the restless winds that blow. . .
And like the wind it too will pass
   and leave nothing more behind

Than the memory of a mystery
    that blew across my mind,
But like the wind it will return
    to keep reminding me
That everything that has been
    is what again will be...
For there is nothing that is new
    beneath God's timeless sun,
And present, past, and future
    are all molded into one.
East and west and north and south—
    the same wind keeps on blowing,
While rivers run on endlessly,
    yet the sea's not overflowing...
And the restless, unknown longing
    of my searching soul won't cease
Until God comes in glory
    and my soul at last finds peace.

—HSR

The Happiness You Already Have

Memories are treasures
    that time cannot destroy,
They are the happy pathway
    to yesterday's bright joy.

                    —HSR

A Mighty Stronghold

Have you ever felt like giving up? The obstacles ahead are too tough and too high for you to overcome. In times like these, God invites you to walk with Him as He reminds you of the many challenges of the past that have come across your path.

Looking back, you remember the time you thought you couldn't make it through, but with God's help, you did. You may recall a heartache you imagined would never stop throbbing, but with the soothing balm of God's comfort and care, it healed. Perhaps a pitfall you stumbled into seemed a disaster at the time, but faith in God's forgiveness gave you the power to carry on.

Yes, obstacles stand in your path, but you aren't meant to face them alone. God, who has been your strength in times past, is your strength and stronghold today.

Remember These Words

We are gathered together on this happy day
To stand before God and to reverently say,
"I take thee to be my partner for life,
To love with and live with
   as husband and wife,
To have and to hold forever, sweetheart,
Through sickness and health,
   until death do us part,
To love and to cherish whatever betide,
And in better or worse to stand by your side."

We do not take this lightly, but solemnly, Lord,
Asking Thy blessing as we live in accord
With Thy holy precepts, which join us in love
And assure us Thy guidance
    and grace from above…
And grant us, dear Lord, that "I will" and "I do"
Are words that grow deeper
    and more meaningful, too,
Through long, happy years
    of caring and sharing,
Secure in the knowledge that we are preparing
A love that is endless and never can die
But finds its fulfillment with You in the sky.

                                    —HSR

Remembrance Road

There is a road I call remembrance
    where I walk each day with you.
It's a pleasant, happy road, my dear,
    all filled with memories true.
Today it leads me through a spot
    where I can dream a while,
And in its tranquil peacefulness
    I touch your hand and smile.
There are hills and fields and budding trees
    and stillness that's so sweet
That it seems that this must be the place
    where God and humans meet.
I hope we can go back again
    and golden hours renew,
And God go with you always, dear,
    until the day we do.

–HSR

Gift of Sharing

God's gift of memory allows us to think back to happy occasions with family and friends, and to remember the many times God has helped us through life's troubles and trials. It's these memories that give us the maturity and wisdom we need to guide and inspire generations to come.

Young people today are meeting life's challenges for the first time. The fears and uncertainties they're experiencing now are many of the same ones you may have faced and overcome. Your listening ear, understanding, and advice can help in more ways than you realize. Their ability to cope with challenge and change comes from the words and example of all who have gone before them.

The special memories you hold in your heart are gifts your years have given to you. And the memories you share are gifts you give to those who need to hear and know.

Somebody Cares

Somebody cares and always will—
The world forgets, but God loves you still.
You cannot go beyond His love
No matter what you're guilty of,
For God forgives until the end—
He is your faithful, loyal friend...
And though you try to hide your face,
There is no shelter any place
That can escape His watchful eye,
For on the earth and in the sky

He's ever-present and always there
To take you in His tender care
And bind the wounds
 and mend the breaks
When all the world around forsakes.
Somebody cares and loves you still,
And God is the someone who always will.

—HSR

There Is No Death

There is no night without a dawning,
 no winter without a spring,
And beyond death's dark horizon
 our hearts once more will sing.
For those who leave us for a while
 have only gone away
Out of a restless, care-worn world
 into a brighter day
Where there will be no partings
 and time is not counted by years,
Where there are no trials or troubles,
 no worries, no cares, and no tears.

—HSR

Poetry Index

About the Author

America's beloved inspirational poet laureate, Helen Steiner Rice, has encouraged millions of people through her beautiful and uplifting verse. Born in Lorain, Ohio, in 1900, Helen was the daughter of a railroad man and an accomplished seamstress and began writing poetry at a young age.

In 1918, Helen began working for a public utilities company and eventually became one of the first female advertising managers and public speakers in the country. In January 1929, she married a wealthy banker named Franklin Rice, who later sank into depression during the Great Depression and eventually committed suicide. Helen later said that her suffering made her sensitive to the pain of others. Her sadness helped her to write some of her most uplifting verses.

Her work for a Cincinnati, Ohio, greeting card company eventually led to her nationwide popularity as a poet when her Christmas card poem "The Priceless Gift of Christmas" was first read on *The Lawrence Welk Show*. Soon Helen had produced several books of her poetry that were a source of inspiration to millions of readers.

Helen died in 1981, leaving a foundation in her name to offer assistance to the needy and the elderly. Now more than thirty years after her death, Helen's words still speak powerfully to the hearts of readers about love and comfort, faith and hope, peace and joy.